Blue Banner Biography

Toby Keith

Amie Jane Leavitt

Mitchell Lane
PUBLISHERS

P.O. Box 196
Hockessin, Delaware 19707
Visit us on the web: www.mitchelllane.com
Comments? email us: mitchelllane@mitchelllane.com

Mitchell Lane PUBLISHERS

Printing   2   3   4   5   6   7   8   9

Blue Banner Biographies

Akon	Alan Jackson	Alicia Keys
Allen Iverson	Ashanti	Ashlee Simpson
Ashton Kutcher	Avril Lavigne	Bernie Mac
Beyoncé	Bow Wow	Brett Favre
Britney Spears	Carrie Underwood	Chris Brown
Chris Daughtry	Christina Aguilera	Christopher Paul Curtis
Ciara	Clay Aiken	Cole Hamels
Condoleezza Rice	Corbin Bleu	Daniel Radcliffe
David Ortiz	Derek Jeter	Eminem
Eve	Fergie (Stacy Ferguson)	50 Cent
Gwen Stefani	Ice Cube	Jamie Foxx
Joe Flacco	John Legend	Ja Rule
Jay-Z	Jennifer Lopez	Jessica Simpson
J. K. Rowling	Johnny Depp	JoJo
Justin Berfield	Justin Timberlake	Kanye West
Kate Hudson	Keith Urban	Kelly Clarkson
Kenny Chesney	Kristen Stewart	Lance Armstrong
Leona Lewis	Lil Wayne	Lindsay Lohan
Mariah Carey	Mario	Mary J. Blige
Mary-Kate and Ashley Olsen	Miguel Tejada	Missy Elliott
Nancy Pelosi	Natasha Bedingfield	Nelly
Orlando Bloom	P. Diddy	Paris Hilton
Peyton Manning	Pink	Queen Latifah
Rihanna	Ron Howard	Rudy Giuliani
Sally Field	Sean Kingston	Selena
Shakira	Shontelle Layne	Soulja Boy Tell 'Em
Taylor Swift	T.I.	Timbaland
Tim McGraw	Toby Keith	Usher
Vanessa Anne Hudgens	Zac Efron	

Library of Congress Cataloging-in-Publication Data
Leavitt, Amie Jane.
  Toby Keith / by Amie Jane Leavitt.
    p. cm. — (Blue banner biographies)
  Discography: p.
  Includes bibliographical references and index.
  ISBN 978-1-58415-678-9 (library bound)
  1. Keith, Toby—Juvenile literature. 2. Country musicians—United States—Biography—Juvenile literature. I. Title.
  ML3930.K35L63 2009
  782.421642092—dc22
  [B]

                                                                          2008008069

ABOUT THE AUTHOR: Amie Jane Leavitt is an accomplished author and photographer. She graduated from Brigham Young University as an education major and has since taught all subjects and grade levels in both private and public schools. She is an adventurer who loves to travel the globe in search of interesting story ideas and beautiful places to capture on film. She has written dozens of books for kids, including biographies on Raven-Symone, Miley Cyrus, and Dylan and Cole Sprouse for Mitchell Lane Publishers. Amie enjoys writing about people who have worked to achieve their dreams. For this reason, she particularly enjoyed researching and writing this book on Toby Keith.

PUBLISHER'S NOTE: The following story has been thoroughly researched, and to the best of our knowledge represents a true story. While every possible effort has been made to ensure accuracy, the publisher will not assume liability for damages caused by inaccuracies in the data, and makes no warranty on the accuracy of the information contained herein. This story has not been authorized or endorsed by Toby Keith.

Blue Banner Biography

Toby Keith performs on his patriotic guitar. After 9/11, his song "Courtesy of the Red, White, and Blue" was especially popular with the U.S. military. Patrick Miller, a prisoner of war in Iraq, even sang the song defiantly to his captors. When Miller returned home to Kansas, Toby sang the song with him in front of Miller's family and friends. Then Toby gave him a flag-motif guitar. "To see big streams going down his face," Toby said, "I just had to hand him that guitar."

Courtesy of the Red, White, and Blue

On a warm summer evening on July 4, 2002, more than 50,000 red-white-and-blue-donned spectators gathered at the LaVell Edwards Stadium in Provo, Utah. They were all coming together to see the annual Stadium of Fire celebration, the largest Independence Day stadium event in the country.

July 4, 2002, was the first Independence Day since the terrorist attacks of September 11, 2001, otherwise known as 9/11. Not only would this Stadium of Fire celebrate the country's freedom, it would also honor the victims and survivors of the terrorist attacks. And since the concert was scheduled to be broadcast to the U.S. troops in Afghanistan, it would honor them as well. Patriotism and camaraderie in the stadium that evening were at an all-time high.

The evening began with the traditional F-16 flyover and the singing of the national anthem while a huge flag was spread out over the football field. Following a few opening acts, the evening's headliner was introduced. The crowd roared when Toby Keith sauntered onto the stage carrying his guitar emblazoned with the stars and stripes.

Many in the stadium that night were delighted he came. "Frankly, I'm surprised," one fan said. "He's the hottest thing in country music right now. That's a big act." Toby's intense patriotism and support of the U.S. troops easily won him the spotlight.

Toby's intense patriotism and support of the U.S. troops easily won him the spotlight.

Toward the end of his concert, he finally played the crowd's most anticipated tune: "Courtesy of the Red, White, and Blue." Before he began, he talked about what the song meant to him and how he had written it for his father, who had died in an automobile accident six months before the terrorist attacks. He felt the song expressed how his father would have felt about the attacks had he been alive to witness them.

"His voice speaks through me today," Toby said, and the crowd applauded in approval. As he started singing, the crowd roared. Video feed from Afghanistan showed the troops singing along with him. The song concluded in impressive style — with a grand pyrotechnic display lighting up the sky behind him.

"I'm glad he did the song," one fan said after the show.

"I personally wanted to come this year because of Toby Keith," another fan commented.

"Courtesy of the Red, White, and Blue" had launched Toby Keith into ultimate stardom. But who was he before he became a big country music star?

Just a Good Ol' Country Boy

Toby Keith's last name isn't Keith. It's actually Covel. When he started his music career, he decided just to use his first and middle names professionally and to drop his surname.

Toby Keith Covel was born in 1961 on July 8 — just a few days after Independence Day. He was the first son and second child of Carolyn Joan Ross Covel and Hubert Keith "H.K." Covel, Jr. His older sister was Tonni. A few years after Toby was born, Carolyn and H.K. would have another son, Tracey.

Toby was born in Clinton, Oklahoma — a small town about 85 miles west of Oklahoma City. The Covels lived there for only a short time before they moved to the outskirts of the capital city. They bought a farm in the community of Moore, Oklahoma. It was on this farm that Toby, Tonni, and Tracey were raised.

H.K. Covel was a hardworking man. "My dad was a regional manager in the oil field service industry for years," Toby said in 1994. H.K. was also very patriotic. "He was a hard-core Democrat, except when it came to the military," Toby said in 2004. H.K. always flew an American flag in front of the Covel home. "That flag just flew — you know, in the '70s, '80s and '90s, it wasn't even real patriotic to wave a flag. . . . He was always just waving the flag about the veterans."

H.K. supported veterans in part because he was one. He had served in the army for two years and was blind in one eye because of an accident during a combat training mission. Toby was seventeen or eighteen years old before he even realized that his dad had only one functional eye. "He was on disability for his whole life and worked in the oil field . . . with one eye [that worked]," Toby said.

Besides a strong work ethic and patriotism, another aspect that Toby shared with his father was a love for country music. At a young age, Toby loved to listen to the musicians who performed at his grandmother's supper club. And at home, he sat around and listened to his dad's favorite country music artists. "I was raised on Hag and Willie . . . and my dad [also] listened to Bob Wills, which was the old Western swing stuff," Toby said.

> *Besides a strong work ethic and patriotism, another aspect that Toby shared with his father was a love for country music.*

Later, Toby would have the honor of singing duets with two of those legends: Merle Haggard and Willie Nelson. In 2002, he sang "Beer for My Horses" with Willie Nelson. Then in 2004, he sang "White Boys" and "She's Not Hooked on Me No More" with Merle Haggard.

Toby performed "Beer for My Horses" with Willie Nelson at the Academy of Country Music Awards in 2003. Toby has been a Willie Nelson fan since he was a child.

When Toby was eight years old, his parents gave him a guitar for Christmas. Toby spent hours teaching himself how to play his new instrument. He never learned how to read music or took any formal lessons. He just learned basic chords and then would play the melodies as he sang along with his favorite country music artists. As his playing improved, he started writing songs of his own.

Not only did Toby love country music, he also liked sports. "I started playing Little League stuff when I was [in] second grade," he said. He played all kinds of sports, including baseball and football. When asked if he was any

After Toby taught himself how to play the guitar, he spent years playing in little bars and clubs throughout Texas and Oklahoma.

good, he replied, "Pretty good. [I'm] still pretty athletic. I think everybody who would play with me would agree."

During high school, he played on the school football team and worked part-time as a rodeo hand. For this job, he helped out in the corral and prepared the animals for their competitions. In his spare time, he continued practicing his music and writing songs.

Oklahoma Oil

*A*fter Toby graduated from Moore High School in 1979, he went to work for his father in the oil business. This wasn't Toby's dream job, but sometimes in life people have to work at jobs that aren't interesting or fun in order to pay the bills. His years spent in the oil fields definitely helped him develop a strong work ethic like his father. As Toby later put it in an interview, "I have worked hard to overcome obstacles in my life and achieve a dream, coming up from working in the oil fields to get where I am in country music."

During his oil-rigging years, Toby started his first band, called Easy Money. He was the lead singer and played guitar and wrote most of the music. The group practiced in the Covel family's barn. Toby and the guys would play their Alabama-style country rock at honky-tonks in the Oklahoma City area. These rundown bars were often frequented by rowdy crowds who tended to get even rowdier as the night wore on. "The places I first played in, if a fight broke out, it could clear the bar. They couldn't afford bouncers, so I'd have to do something to keep from losing my audience. If I saw a big fight fixing to happen, I'd put down my guitar and jump off the stage. I'm six-foot-four, 235 pounds . . . that's a great advantage," he said.

After he worked for a few years in the oil fields, he decided to try something new. He tried out for the Oklahoma City Drillers—a semiprofessional team that was part of the old United States Football League. Toby made the team and played defensive end. His build was perfect for this position, and he played for two years.

Meanwhile, Toby continued playing his music at local dance halls and bars on the weekends. But one weekend night, he wasn't performing. He was just at the dance hall as a customer on one of his few nights off. That's when he met his future wife, Tricia. He had seen her at other times when he was playing onstage, but this was the first time they really got the chance to talk. Shortly after that, the two started dating. They were married in 1984. Tricia already had a child, a daughter named Shelley, when the two met. Toby adopted Shelley and raised her as his own. He and Tricia would have two more children—a daughter, Krystal, born in 1984, and a son, Stelen Keith, born in 1997.

"If I saw a big fight fixing to happen, I'd put down my guitar and jump off the stage. I'm six-foot-four, 235 pounds."

After playing for years with Easy Money, the group finally reached a point where they had to make a decision. "We finally one day just come to a crossroad and said, 'You know what? We need to take this thing on the road and find out what we got,' " he said. They felt they had done all they could do locally with their music, and if they wanted to be successful in the industry, they would have to reach out to a wider audience.

In 1984, they started playing in little bars and clubs throughout Oklahoma and Texas and as far north as Colorado. Soon they were on the road for 51 weeks out of a year, giving them only one week at home to spend with their families. This must have been hard for Toby, a devoted family man who loves his wife and kids a great deal. But he felt he had to make these sacrifices if he wanted to be a full-time musician. "It was the only way we could make enough money," he said. "Nothing [is] worth having if it's not worth fighting for."

Toby and the guys kept up the grueling schedule for seven years. They knew they couldn't just keep playing at little honky-tonks forever. They would eventually need to get signed to a record company if they wanted to get on the radio and get bigger gigs. If that didn't happen soon, they would just have to call it quits and head back to the Oklahoma oil fields and get "real jobs."

In 1992, the group made a demo tape featuring some of their most popular songs, and they took it to all the major

> *Soon they were on the road for 51 weeks out of a year, giving them only one week at home to spend with their families.*

Harold Shedd (right) gave Toby and Easy Money their big break in 1992. The two remained good friends for many years.

recording studios in Nashville. No one was interested. In fact, one of the major record executives said their songs were not "Nashville quality."

Although the band might have been discouraged by this, they kept right on playing. Finally, they got a break. When they were performing in Oklahoma, Harold Shedd, the president of Mercury Records, was in the audience. He had once been the producer of the hit band Alabama, so he knew talent when he saw it. He really liked what he heard from Toby Keith and his band, and he offered them a recording contract.

Should've Been a Cowboy

*O*nce Toby's music hit the airwaves, it became a nationwide success. In 1993, his first album, titled *Toby Keith*, was released. It was certified platinum, which means it sold more than a million copies. In fact, it sold well over two million.

The biggest hit on the album was the song "Should've Been a Cowboy." It topped the country music charts, spending two weeks at number one. Eventually this song would become the most played country music single of the entire 1990s. Five other songs on the album also made the top five on the charts, including "I Didn't Know Now," "A Little Less Talk and a Lot More Action," and "He Ain't Worth Missing."

Shortly after Toby signed with Mercury, Harold Shedd moved on to Polydor Records. Toby and the guys decided to go with him. It was at Polydor that Toby released his next two albums: *Boomtown* in 1995 and *Blue Moon* in 1996. *Boomtown* went gold (which means it sold more than 500,000 copies), and *Blue Moon* went platinum. *Boomtown* included another number one hit, titled "Who's That Man," and a Top 5 hit, titled "You Ain't Much Fun."

Toby was performing in Oklahoma City when he got the news about "Who's That Man" hitting the top of the chart. He was excited not only for the success of his album but also because it was the first number one for the new Polydor label. "It's a good way to kick off a new album," he said.

Even though Toby was achieving a great deal of success, he still tried to stay grounded. "I'm pretty much a Wal-Mart kind of guy," he said in a radio interview. "I have a nice home and material things, but my children go to public schools and we act pretty normal." He wanted people to know that just because he was successful, he wasn't going to change. "The story will be how I was after I became successful, not how I became successful," he said.

One of the most exciting things about becoming successful was that he could spend his money to help important people in his life. "Music has let me do things for people," he said. "My dad was a regional manager in the oil field service industry for years, and he tried to start his own [oil] business. I bought him a company, and he's doing what he always wanted."

Toby's success was definitely hard-earned. In order to promote his music, he had to be out on the road a lot. Between 1992 and 1994, he traveled to every state except Oregon, Alaska, and Hawaii. It was likely very difficult for both Toby and his family to be apart so much.

> "I'm pretty much a Wal-Mart kind of guy," he said. "I have a nice home and material things, but . . . we act pretty normal."

In 1996, the same year he released *Blue Moon*, Toby was asked by the Beach Boys to sing on the album *Beach Boys' Stars and Stripes Vol. 1*. He sang "Be True to Your School," which had been one of the Beach Boys' big hits of 1961. As Toby sang this song, the Beach Boys sang the harmony and backup vocals for him. Toby probably never imagined that he would have the Beach Boys—a group that was popular the year he was born—as his backup singers.

Polydor eventually closed its Nashville offices, and Toby returned to Mercury. In 1997, he released his next album, *Dream Walkin'*. On this album, Toby sings a duet titled "I'm So Happy I Can't Stop Crying" with British artist Sting. For this song, Toby and Sting were nominated for a Grammy. The two were then invited to sing the duet at the 1997 Country Music Association Awards. In 1998, Toby released his *Greatest Hits* album.

In 1999, Toby decided to move from Mercury to DreamWorks Nashville. It was with this label that he released *How Do You Like Me Now?* The most popular song on the album, which shares the same title, topped the charts, spending five weeks at number one. Album sales went through the roof. Soon, the album was certified double-platinum.

In 2000, Toby won two Academy of Country Music Awards—one for Male Vocalist of the Year and the other for Best Album. The following year, he won his first CMA

> *Toby probably never imagined that he would have the Beach Boys as his backup singers.*

Most people probably thought that Toby and British artist Sting were an unlikely pair. But the duo's song "I'm So Happy I Can't Stop Crying" won them a Grammy nomination in 1997. The two also performed the song together at the 1997 CMA Awards telecast.

(Country Music Association) award for Best Male Vocalist and was nominated for six Academy of Country Music awards.

In 2001, he released *Pull My Chain*. He wrote nine of the thirteen tracks on the album. Three of them became number-one hits: "I'm Just Talking About Tonight," "I Wanna Talk About Me," and "My List."

This album was particularly special for Toby because he dedicated it to the memory of his dad. On March 24, 2001,

Toby Keith uses many of his life experiences when he writes his songs. One example is "How Do You Like Me Now?" Toby told a newspaper reporter once, " 'How do you like me now?' is something I always said when playing football after I knocked someone down."

On October 4, 2000, Toby brought his wife, Tricia, and son, Stelen Keith, to the 34th Annual CMA Awards in Nashville. Toby was one of the performers for this Grand Old Opry event, which was viewed by over 38 million people on CBS. The following year, in 2001, Toby was named CMA's Male Vocalist of the Year.

H.K. was driving along I-35, the main highway that goes through Oklahoma City. His truck was sideswiped by another vehicle and was pushed off the road and into the median. When it came up on the other side into oncoming traffic, it was struck by a charter bus with faulty brakes. H.K. was killed. He was only sixty-four years old.

This was an extremely difficult time for Toby and his family. Toby had been very close to his dad, and he missed him greatly. He struggled with coming to terms with his dad's death for many months.

Ultimate Stardom

On September 11, 2001, Toby was in Louisville, Kentucky, purchasing some Thoroughbred horses at a horse sale. He remembers it clearly, because that's where he was when he heard about the attacks at the World Trade Center and the Pentagon and the crash of Flight 93 in the fields of Pennsylvania. Like the rest of the country, Toby was shocked by the events of that day. A few days later, he was at home, working out in his gym. He started thinking about his dad's patriotism and what his dad would think if he were still around.

Toby grabbed a fantasy football roster that he and his band had lying around. "I just ripped one of those and flipped it over and just went to writing a bunch of lyrics down. And they're sideways and up across the top. And when I was done, I just pieced it together," he said. The end result was the song "Courtesy of the Red, White, and Blue."

"That song was so big and struck such a chord," says Toby. "It peeled the layers off and brought out the true colors people had. But I never intended to record this. I really wanted it as an honor and tribute to my dad. I wanted to go out and sing it to military people. Here's something that I wrote for you guys, for your duty."

Toby began playing the song at a few select concerts for military personnel. After one of the concerts near the Pentagon, he was approached by General James L. Jones, a Marine Corps commander. He said, "You know what? We need this song. . . . You can do me a huge favor and . . . release it right now. Just stick it out and let everybody hear it. They'll play it."

General James L. Jones told Toby, "We need this song. . . . You can do me a huge favor and . . . release it right now."

Toby thought about it for a while. He prayed about it. He talked to his family and his manager. He knew it would be a controversial song, but he decided to do as the general had asked.

Toby was right. Some people loved the song and other people hated it. Originally, Toby had a confirmed invitation to perform on *ABC*'s *Fourth of July Celebration with Peter Jennings*. But because Jennings didn't like the song, he asked that Toby either play something else or change the lyrics. Toby refused, and the invitation was revoked. Later, Natalie Maines from the Dixie Chicks remarked that the song "makes country music sound ignorant."

Toby just let these comments go, but they still hurt because the song was written in memory of his father. "You know, I just have never been one to criticize other people's music," he said.

On November 9, 2004, Toby and his daughter, Krystal, sang together at the 38th Annual CMA Awards. The two rocked Nashville's Grand Ole Opry House with their duet, "Mockingbird."

Even though there was some backlash for his song, the number of fans far outweighed the critics. Members of the military particularly loved it. The words "Courtesy of the Red, White, and Blue" were written on bombs and armored vehicles in both Afghanistan and Iraq. In fact, "the tank that took down the statue in Saddam Hussein City, with him on the horse and everything, [the tank's nickname] was Courtesy of the Red, White, and Blue," Toby said. He never imagined that his song would have that much of an effect on the military and the American public.

In 2002, Toby released *Unleashed*; its first track is "Courtesy of the Red, White, and Blue." Selling 338,000 copies during its first week, the album became the number one country album and number one pop album in the nation.

In 2003, Toby and Willie Nelson were asked to open the Academy of Country Music Awards ceremony with their song "Beer for My Horses." After the performance, they slipped out to the tour bus to finish a song they were working on. Toby had been nominated for the Entertainer of the Year award, but he didn't think he had a chance to win, so he didn't worry about sticking around. When they read his name as the winner, he wasn't around to accept it! "I didn't feel like we had a chance to win anything, coming in. That was the vibe we were catching. I'm pretty shocked about it," he told a reporter.

In August 2005, Toby decided to start his own record label, which he named Show Dog Nashville.

From 2003 to 2005, Toby released three more albums with DreamWorks: *Shock'n Ya'll* in 2003, *Greatest Hits 2* in 2004, and *Honkytonk University* in 2005. On *Greatest Hits 2*, Toby performed "Mockingbird" with his daughter Krystal. "Krystal is an incredible singer, and it is just as good as it gets to work with her. She did a great job on the song and I am so proud of her," he said.

In August 2005, Toby decided to start his own record label, which he named Show Dog Nashville. His first release on his label was his album *White Trash with Money*, which came out in 2006. The following year, he released *Big Dog Daddy*. That year, he also performed in his first Hollywood movie, *Broken Bridges*.

Toby is passionate about performing for good causes. He has gone on numerous USO tours to places such as Cuba,

Toby has played for hundreds of servicemen and women on USO tours around the world. After one of the tours, Toby said about the troops, "I have a whole new respect for the people that are away. They're over there, away from their families for a year, a year and a half at a time and they're not sure if they're coming back. It just puts a smile on their face when they see America show up."

Belgium, Germany, Iraq, and Afghanistan. After the concerts, he'll spend hours signing autographs for the men and women in the military. Toby says that the best part about being on a USO tour is "just being able to bring a part of America over to them."

Toby also believes in supporting worthwhile causes. He set up the Toby Keith Foundation, which benefits charitable organizations—particularly those that help kids with cancer. He holds an annual golf tournament that helps raise money for these causes.

He set up the Toby Keith Foundation, which benefits charitable organizations—particularly those that help kids with cancer.

Toby loves living on his 160-acre horse farm in Norman, Oklahoma, with his wife and kids. He loves the local community and has even opened a restaurant in the Bricktown district to help attract crowds and dollars to the area. Fittingly, it's called Toby Keith's I Love This Bar and Grill, after his 2003 hit "I Love This Bar."

Unlike other country stars, Toby doesn't plan on moving to Nashville. "I'd trade every nomination to stay right where I'm at, with my family and my roots," he says. He is good friends with people he's known since his childhood. He coaches his son's football team. He raises and breeds horses on his ranch. "I'm always going to be a country boy," he says.

Even though Toby loves performing and singing his music, he actually loves writing it more. Most singers do not write their own music; they sing other people's songs. Not Toby. He considers himself a singer/songwriter. In fact,

Operation One Voice, which benefits families of fallen Special Operations Forces members, presented Toby with a plaque and other gifts to thank him for all he does for police officers, firefighters, and U.S. military troops.

most of the songs on his albums were written or cowritten by him. "Music is such a God-given thing to me," he says. "Songwriting is my one talent in the world that outshines all of my other talents. It's such an easy process for me to write a song. That's what I'm good at. That is my gift," he says.

And hopefully, for Toby's fans worldwide, he'll go right on writing and singing for many years to come. After all, that's *how we like him now*!

1961   Toby Keith Covel is born in Clinton, Oklahoma, on July 8.

1969   He starts playing team sports; receives his first guitar for Christmas.

1979   He graduates from Moore High School. He begins working in oil fields.

1981   He starts the band Easy Money.

1982   He plays semiprofessional football.

1984   He marries Tricia and adopts her daughter, Shelley; Tricia and Toby have their first child together, daughter Krystal.

1992   Toby and his band, Easy Money, take a demo tape to Nashville recording studios; they sign with Mercury Records.

1993   The album *Toby Keith* is released.

1994   The band moves with Harold Shedd to Polydor Records.

1995   *Boomtown* is released.

1996   *Blue Moon* is released. Toby sings "Be True to Your School" with the Beach Boys.

1997   Toby and Tricia's son, Stelen Keith, is born. *Dream Walkin'* is released by Mercury Records. Toby sings "I'm So Happy I Can't Stop Crying" with Sting at the Country Music Awards.

1998   *Greatest Hits 1* is released.

1999   Toby moves to the DreamWorks Nashville record label and releases the album *How Do You Like Me Now?*

2000   Toby receives the Academy of Country Music's Male Vocalist of the Year and Best Album awards.

2001   He receives the Country Music Association's Male Vocalist of the Year award and is nominated for six Academy of Country Music awards; *Pull My Chain* is released; Toby's father is killed in an automobile accident in March. Toby writes "Courtesy of the Red, White, and Blue" in response to terrorist attacks of September 11.

2002   *Unleashed* is released. Toby performs at the Stadium of Fire in Provo, Utah, on July 4.

2003   *Shock'n Ya'll* is released. Toby performs "Beer for My Horses" with Willie Nelson at the Academy of Country Music Awards ceremony and is absent when his name is announced as the winner of the academy's Entertainer of the Year award.

2004   *Greatest Hits 2* is released. Toby sings "Mockingbird" on this album with his daughter Krystal. He sings "White Boys" and "She's Not Hooked on Me No More" with Merle Haggard.

2005   *Honkytonk University* is released. Toby starts his record label, Show Dog Nashville. He opens the first Toby Keith's I Love This Bar and Grill in Oklahoma City.

2006   *White Trash with Money* is released. Toby appears in his first Hollywood movie, *Broken Bridges*.

2007   *Big Dog Daddy* is released.

2008   He appears in *Beer for My Horses*. He releases his album *That Don't Make Me a Bad Guy* in October.

2009   He begins working on the movie *Provinces of Night* with Hilary Duff.

Albums

2008	*That Don't Make Me a Bad Guy*
	Toby Keith's 35 Biggest Hits
2007	*Big Dog Daddy*
	A Classic Christmas
2006	*White Trash with Money*
2005	*Honkytonk University*
2004	*Greatest Hits 2*
2003	*20th-Century Masters – The Millennium Collection: The Best of Toby Keith*
	Shock'n Ya'll
2002	*Unleashed*
2001	*Pull My Chain*
1999	*How Do You Like Me Now?*
1998	*Greatest Hits 1*
1997	*Dream Walkin'*
1996	*Blue Moon*
1995	*Boomtown*
	Christmas to Christmas
1993	*Toby Keith*

Singles

2009	"God Love Her"
2008	"She's a Hottie"
2007	"High Maintenance Woman"
2006	"Crash Here Tonight," "A Little Too Late"
2005	"As Good As I Once Was"
2002	"Beer for My Horses" (with Willie Nelson)
2001	"I Wanna Talk About Me"
2000	"How Do You Like Me Now?"
1998	"Getcha Some"
1997	"I'm So Happy I Can't Stop Crying," "We Were In Love"
1996	"Closin' Time at Home," "Does That Blue Moon Ever Shine On You"
1995	"You Ain't Much Fun," "Upstairs Downtown"
1994	"Who's That Man"
1993	"A Little Less Talk and a Lot More Action," "He Ain't Worth Missing," "Should've Been a Cowboy"

FILMOGRAPHY

2008   *Beer for My Horses*
2006   *Broken Bridges*

FURTHER READING

Books

If you enjoyed this biography of Toby Keith, you might also enjoy these other country music Blue Banner Biographies from Mitchell Lane Publishers:

Adams, Michelle Medlock. *Kenny Chesney*. Hockessin, Delaware: Mitchell Lane Publishers, 2007.

Adams, Michelle Medlock. *Tim McGraw*. Hockessin, Delaware: Mitchell Lane Publishers, 2007.

Leavitt, Amie Jane. *Keith Urban*. Hockessin, Delaware: Mitchell Lane Publishers, 2008.

Reusser, Kayleen. *Taylor Swift*. Hockessin, Delaware: Mitchell Lane Publishers, 2009.

Torres, Jennifer. *Alan Jackson*. Hockessin, Delaware: Mitchell Lane Publishers, 2007.

Tracy, Kathleen. *Carrie Underwood*. Hockessin, Delaware: Mitchell Lane Publishers, 2006.

Works Consulted

"The Best of Toby Keith." PR Newswire. April 14, 2003.
    http://www.accessmylibrary.com/coms2/summary_0286-22984185_ITM

Bisbee, Julie E. "Toby Keith Doesn't Stray Far from Oklahoma Roots." The America's Intelligence Wire. November 19, 2004.
    http://www.accessmylibrary.com/coms2/summary_0286-14527088_ITM

CMT Artist Page: "Toby Keith."
    http://www.cmt.com/artists/az/keith_toby/artist.jhtml

"Country's Toby Keith Top ACM Award Winner." UPI NewsTrack Entertainment News. May 27, 2004.
    http://www.accessmylibrary.com/coms2/summary_0286-7072547_ITM

Crawford, Greg. "Country Singer Toby Keith Is a Very Vocal Patriot." Knight Ridder Newspapers.
    http://www.accessmylibrary.com/coms2/summary_0286-7394154_ITM

"Encore Presentation: Interview with Country Singer Toby Keith—Part 1 and 2" Cnn.com—Larry King Live, The America's Intelligence Wire. January 31, 2004.
    http://www.accessmylibrary.com/coms2/summary_0286-20183786_ITM
    http://www.accessmylibrary.com/coms2/summary_0286-20093674_ITM

Entenmann, Dalene. "Toby Keith: Golf and Music for Kids with Cancer," May 1, 2006. http://www.thecancerblog.com/2006/05/01/
    toby-keith-golf-and-music-for-kids-with-cancer/

"Ford Truck Ads Featuring Toby Keith Premiere on Monday Night Football."
   Business Wire. October 7, 2002.
   http://www.accessmylibrary.com/coms2/summary_0286-26166933_ITM

Hayes, John. " 'White Trash with Money' Country Star Toby Keith Wears the Label
   with Pride." *Pittsburgh Post-Gazette*, September 3, 2006.
   http://archive.southcoasttoday.com/daily/09-06/09-03-06/01living.htm

"Merle Haggard, Toby Keith Duet Set." UPI News Track, *Entertainment News*.
   August 17, 2004.
   http://www.accessmylibrary.com/coms2/summary_0286-8714899_ITM

Nash, Alanna. "Red, White and Cowboy Blues." *USA Weekend*. November 2, 2003.
   http://www.usaweekend.com/03_issues/031102/031102toby_keith.html

Samms, Diane Rush. "Family Is the Top Priority for Up-and-Coming Singer Toby
   Keith." Knight-Ridder/Tribune News Service. October 20, 1994.
   http://www.accessmylibrary.com/coms2/summary_0286-5526405_ITM

Tarradell, Mario. "Alan Jackson Lamented the Heart While Toby Keith Sought
   the Blood." *The Dallas Morning News*, Knight Ridder/Tribune News Service,
   September 6, 2002.
   http://www.accessmylibrary.com/coms2/summary_0286-7409886_ITM

Tarradell, Mario. "Reviews of New Releases from Toby Keith and Pepe Aguilar." *The
   Dallas Morning News*. Knight-Ridder/Tribune News Service. August 23, 2001.
   http://www.accessmylibrary.com/coms2/summary_0286-7874323_ITM

"Toby Keith" USO.
   http://www.uso.org/search/default.aspx?word=toby+keith

"Toby Keith Biography." Billboard.com.
   http://www.billboard.com/bbcom/bio/index.jsp?pid=32325

"Toby Keith Biography." MTV.com.
   http://www.mtv.com/music/artist/keith_toby/artist.jhtml#bio

"Toby Keith: Good As Ever." CBS News. June 22, 2005.
   http://www.cbsnews.com/stories/2005/06/22/earlyshow/series/
   summer_concerts/main703408.shtml

"Toby Keith Named to Hall of Fame." *The Norman Transcript*.
   http://www.normantranscript.com/moorenews/local_story_150012331

On the Internet

Toby Keith Official Website
   http://tobykeith.musiccitynetworks.com/

CMT.com: Toby Keith
   http://www.cmt.com/artists/az/keith_toby/artist.jhtml

MySpace: Toby Keith
   http://www.myspace.com/tobykeith

Great American Country: Toby Keith
   http://www.gactv.com/gac/ar_az_toby_keith/article/
   0,,GAC_26115_4703433,00.html

INDEX